From Egg to Adult
The Life Cycle of Fish

Richard and Louise
Spilsbury

Heinemann Library
Chicago, Illinois

Customer Service 888-454-2279
Visit our website at www.heinemannlibrary.com

Editing, Design, Photo Research, and Production by Heinemann Library
Illustrations by David Woodroffe
Originated by Dot Gradations Ltd
Printed in China by Wing King Tong

07 06 05 04 03
10 9 8 7 6 5 4 3 2 1

Library of Congress Cataloging-in-Publication Data
Spilsbury, Louise.
    The life cycle of fish / Louise & Richard Spilsbury.
       p. cm. -- (From egg to adult)
    Summary: Discusses how fish differ from other animals, their habitat, how they are born and develop, what they eat, how they reproduce, and their typical life expectancy.
    Includes bibliographical references and index.
    ISBN 1-4034-0783-5 (HC) 1-4034-3405-0 (PB)
    1. Fishes--Life cycles--Juvenile literature.   [1. Fishes.]
    I. Spilsbury, Richard. II. Title. III. Series.
    QL617.2.S687 2003
    597--dc21
                                    2002011708

Acknowledgments
The Publishers would like to thank the following for permission to reproduce photographs:
p. 4 NHPA/Lutra; p. 5 Bruce Coleman Collection/Kim Taylor; p. 6 Oxford Scientific Films/Rodger Jackman; p. 7 NHPA; p. 8 Heather Angel; pp. 9, 26 (top) Corbis/Natalie Fobes; p. 10 Oxford Scientific Films/Breck P. Kent; p. 11 SPL; pp. 12, 15 NHPA/Ant Photo Library; p. 13 Oxford Scientific Films/Colin Milkins; p. 14 Oxford Scientific Films/David Fleetham; p. 16 Oxford Scientific Films/Karen Gowlett-Holmes; p. 17 Bruce Coleman; p. 18 Oxford Scientific Films/Ian Root; pp. 19, 28 Corbis; p. 20 FLPA/C. J. Swale; p. 21 Oxford Scientific Films/Clive Bromhall; p. 22 NHPA/Kevin Schafer; p. 23 Oxford Scientific Films/Howard Hall; p. 24 FLPA/D. P. Wilson; p. 25 Bruce Coleman Collection/Jeff Foott; p. 26 (bottom) NHPA/Trevor Mcdonald; p. 27 Oxford Scientific Films.

Cover photograph of the golden Mozambique mouth brooder is reproduced with permission of Oxford Scientific Films.

The fish at the top of each page is a blue French angelfish.

Every effort has been made to contact copyright holders of any material reproduced in this book. Any omissions will be rectified in subsequent printings if notice is given to the Publishers.

Some words are shown in bold, **like this.** You can find out what they mean by looking in the glossary.

Contents

Look but don't touch: Many fish are easily hurt, and some are dangerous. If you see one in the wild, do not get too close to it. Look at it, but do not try to touch it!

What Is a Fish?

There are about 23,000 different kinds, or **species,** of fish in the world. Although they may look very different, they share certain features that make them all fish. All fish are **vertebrates,** which means that they have backbones. They live in water and breathe through special body parts called **gills.** Fish are cold-blooded. That means they cannot control their body temperature. It changes as the temperature of the water around them changes.

This is a perch, one of the most common kinds of fish. Like most fish, it is covered with **scales** *that protect its body.*

Where do fish live?

All fish live in water. Water is harder to move through than air, so fish are shaped to help them swim. Most are streamlined—that is, they have smooth body shapes that can move through water quickly. They swim by moving their bodies from side to side. They use their **fins** for braking and keeping themselves upright and steady.

How Are Fish Born?

Most baby fish hatch from eggs laid by their mother. A female fish produces many eggs at a time, but the exact number depends on her health and the species she belongs to. For example, sticklebacks usually lay about 200 eggs, but turbots can lay 9 million eggs.

This picture of a fish egg has been made bigger so that you can see the embryo inside.

What's in a fish egg?

The baby fish growing inside an egg is called an **embryo.** Fish eggs, like those of other animals, contain a bag of food called the **yolk.** The embryo uses this food to give it **energy** to grow bigger and stronger. Fish eggs do not have a shell as do bird and reptile eggs. Most fish eggs have a thin coating that provides little protection for the growing embryo.

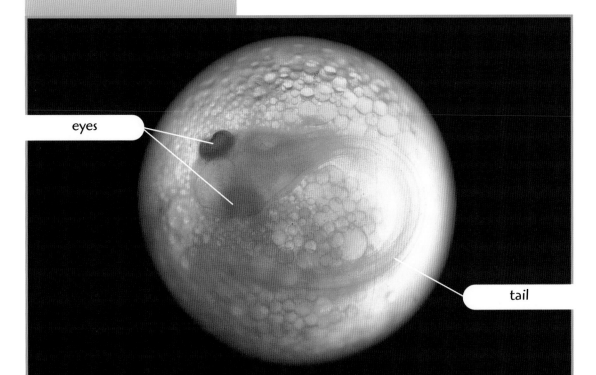

eyes

tail

Where are fish born?

Almost all fish eggs hatch in water. Some float one by one at the water's surface and are spread by the tides. Others are sticky and sink to the bottom, where they cling to plants and rocks. Some fish lay their eggs in big clumps or in long strings.

Pacific herrings lay their sticky eggs in shallow water in spring. These eggs are stuck to seaweed.

Odd ones out

Some fish, such as guppies, do not lay eggs. They give birth to live young. The **embryos** develop and the eggs hatch inside the female's body. Because there is not much room inside a fish's body, these fish have only a few young at a time.

How long does hatching take?

Embryos of different fish take different lengths of time to develop before they are ready to hatch. Most fish eggs hatch after about two months, but some tropical fish eggs hatch after only a day or two. Shark eggs can take up to five months to hatch. The speed can depend on water temperature. If the same kinds of eggs are laid in warmer water, they hatch more quickly than those in colder water.

How do fish hatch?

When the embryo inside an egg is fully developed, it wriggles and squirms until it breaks open its egg's coating. A newly hatched fish is often called a **fry.** Fry of many types of fish often hatch around the same time because their eggs were laid at the same time.

Brown trout fry, such as this one, are ready to hatch two to four months after the eggs are laid.

Who Takes Care of Baby Fish?

Most fish never see their parents. After laying the eggs, the parents have nothing more to do with them. The **fry** that hatch have to take care of themselves. Newly hatched fish are usually very small. Adult plaice are about 20 inches (50 centimeters) long, but their fry only measure $1/4$ inch (6.5 millimeters). The **muscles** and **fins** that will help them swim are not fully grown.

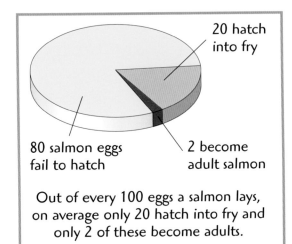

20 hatch into fry

80 salmon eggs fail to hatch

2 become adult salmon

Out of every 100 eggs a salmon lays, on average only 20 hatch into fry and only 2 of these become adults.

Most fry, such as this one, do not live for many days after hatching because of predators.

Countdown!

There is an important reason why fish lay so many eggs. The fry that hatch are often very small, and **predators** feed on them in large numbers. Laying lots of eggs helps make sure that at least a few fry will grow into adults.

Alone is risky

Life is dangerous for young fish. Because they cannot swim well, they may be washed into colder waters or away from food. Their weakness also makes them easy to catch, and many different predators, including insects, fish, birds, and frogs, try to eat them. Many kinds of fish fry hide to avoid being seen.

Model parents

Some fish take care of their fry. After she lays her eggs, the female tilapia takes them into her mouth. The eggs hatch, and the fry stay in her mouth until they are big enough to take care of themselves. The males of a few **species,** such as some sticklebacks, guard their fry for a short time after they have hatched.

Coho salmon hatch at night. This gives them a chance to swim to the shelter of shady pools and banks before daylight. There they can feed hidden from predators.

How Do Baby Fish Grow Bigger?

Young fish must eat food to get the **energy** that their bodies need to grow bigger. When most fish first hatch, they look quite different from the adult. Many have unformed **fins** and they still have a **yolk sac** attached to their stomach. They live off food from this sac until it is all used up. By this time, they are able to find food for themselves.

The fins on this trout fry are not yet fully formed, and it has a yolk sac on its stomach. The yolk lasts until the fins are fully grown. This takes about three to four months.

Name-calling

People give fish particular names for the different stages of growth. When salmon hatch out they are called alevins. At four to six weeks old, they start to eat insect **larvae,** and become **fry.** Two years later, they develop stripes and are called parrs. After another two years they lose the stripes and become silver smolts. As adults, they are reddish-brown with red and black spots.

First foods

Young fish usually eat small bits of food that float in the water. This food may be tiny plants and insect eggs or larvae. As they get bigger, fish need to eat larger amounts of food. Young anglerfish live at the surface of the ocean at first, eating **plankton.** When they become adults, they move to the deep sea to eat other fish and squid.

Some fish eat plankton all their lives, from fry to adult. They just eat a lot more of it as they grow. Plankton eaters include two of the biggest fish of all—the basking shark and the whale shark. These huge fish swim along with their mouths open, catching tons of plankton.

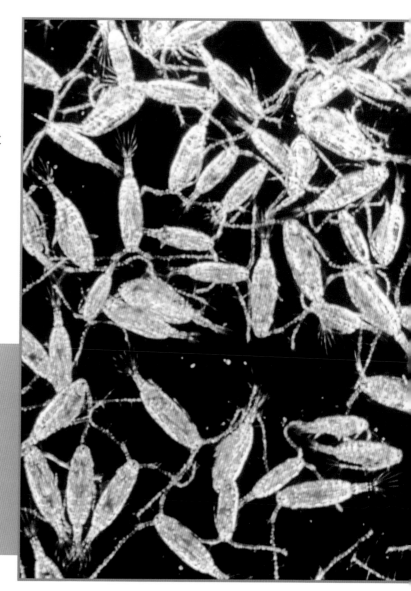

Many baby ocean fish eat tiny floating animals, such as these copepods. There are several different types of copepods, and most are about the size of two of the periods at the end of this sentence.

The whale shark is a huge **plankton** eater with a mouth the size of a bathtub. As it swims, hundreds of quarts or liters of water flow into its mouth and pass over its **gills.** This water contains floating plankton, which are trapped by rows of bristles called gill rakers and then swallowed.

On the menu

Some of the fish that live in rivers and streams eat plants that grow on the banks and river bottoms. Others eat the small animals that feed on those plants, such as snails and worms, or insects and other fish. Out in the deep oceans and seas, there are no plants to eat, so most fish are **carnivores.** Some feed on plankton. Others eat shrimps, crabs, **shellfish,** or other fish.

Hunters

Most meat-eating fish hunt for their **prey.** Tuna and barracuda swim swiftly into large **schools** of fish to catch a meal. Swordfish spear and slash their prey with a long, pointed, swordlike snout. Electric eels stun their prey with electric shocks. Pike hide behind sea plants and charge out to catch prey with their sharp teeth.

Pike eat almost anything they can catch—fish, frogs, birds, and sometimes even young otters.

Unusual food

Some fish are **scavengers.** They do not catch their own meals, but eat dead animals that sink down to the bottom. Hagfish are scavengers. They have rough tongues that can scrape the flesh off dead animals. Some fish eat different things at different times of year. The arapaima fish in the Amazon eats fish most of the time. When the forest is flooded and it finds itself swimming among trees, it eats fruit.

*Some fish eat only one type of food. This parrotfish eats only coral from a **coral reef.** It scrapes off bits of coral using the hard teeth in its beaklike mouth.*

Senses

Fish use different senses for finding food. Pike have very good eyesight to spot prey. Great white sharks can trace tiny amounts of blood from dead or injured animals hundreds of yards or meters away. Catfish have **barbels,** which are fleshy feelers that look like a cat's whiskers. They use these to "taste" the water to find crabs and other shellfish to eat.

How Do Fish Grow Up Safely?

One way that fish avoid the many **predators** that try to eat them is by using **camouflage**—shapes, patterns, or colors on their bodies that help them blend into the background so that predators do not notice them.

In disguise

Some fish are simply colored like the rocks they swim and rest among. Flatfish and rays are sandy colored. They also have flat bodies that make them very hard to see when they lie on the ocean floor. Most fish are darker on top than on their belly. When a predator below looks up, the fish's pale belly cannot easily be seen against the light from the sky. From above, its dark back makes it hard to see against the darker water below.

It is almost impossible to spot the sea dragon, a kind of seahorse. The shape, color, and flaps of skin on this unusual fish make it look like floating seaweed!

Defenses

Many fish use built-in defenses to protect them against predators. Some have armor made of tough **scales** or plates over their bodies. Weever fish have spiky **fins** that shoot poison into anything that touches them. Electric eels give their enemies a nasty electric shock.

Clownfish hide among the long, snakelike, stinging tentacles of sea anemones in a coral reef. They do not get stung because their bodies are covered in a special protective slime, and **predators** leave them alone because of the tentacles.

The pufferfish has scales shaped like spikes. To keep predators away, this fish blows itself up with air into a scary spiky ball!

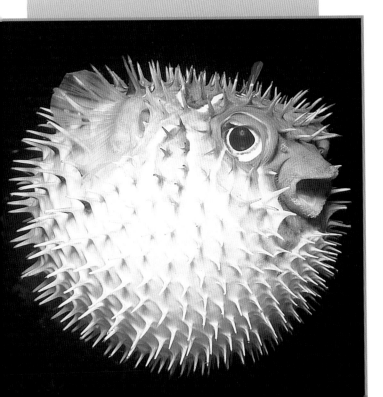

Different scales

Some fish, such as catfish, have tough, leathery skin. Most fish have scales to protect the soft skin beneath.

Scales come in all shapes and sizes. Carp have rounded scales that overlap like the tiles on a roof. Perch have scales with jagged "teeth" on one end.

Keeping out of the way

As they grow, fish learn to keep out of the way of predators. Some do this by hiding. Sand eels dig into the sand, and some gobies live in holes made by prawns. Some fish escape danger by making a quick getaway. With its fins folded in, the sailfish is shaped like a smooth dart. It can shoot through the water at speeds of up to about 70 miles (110 kilometers) per hour.

Flying fish have a unique way of getting away from predators. They open their big side fins like wings and glide swiftly over the surface of the water.

Safety in numbers

About one-fifth of all **species** of fish swim in **schools** for protection. Anchovies and herrings form particularly large schools. When a predator attacks, it is confused about which fish to take, and so it catches fewer than it could if the **prey** swam in smaller groups.

Avoiding the cold

In some places, the fresh water in rivers and ponds freezes in winter. To survive, some pond fish, such as goldfish, stop feeding and move to the bottom of the pond where the water is warmer. Some river fish **migrate** to warmer, deeper waters during winter.

A lungfish can survive for up to four years in its nest. It comes out when rain fills the pond again.

Sheltering from the heat

When heat makes ponds dry up, most fish die because they cannot breathe out of water. African lungfish have lungs as well as gills. They dig down into the mud in the drying pond and make a nest of slime around themselves. This keeps them moist as the mud around them bakes hard. They leave a narrow tunnel to the surface, and use their lungs to breathe air through it.

When Is a Fish Grown Up?

A fish is "grown up" when it is ready to start **breeding**—when it is able to **reproduce** and have young of its own. Some **species** of fish take longer to become adults than others. Most small fish, such as guppies, are grown up a few months after hatching, but whale sharks take about 25 years to become adults!

Other things, such as temperature and the fight for food, also change the speed at which a fish grows. For example, if a tropical fish that usually lives in warm, shallow waters drifts into cooler, deeper seas, it may grow more slowly than its relatives. If many fish that are **carnivores** live in an area with a small amount of **prey,** the fish may grow more slowly because they have less to eat.

The great white shark is grown up at about 10 years of age. It may live for 30 years and reach a length of 23 feet (7 meters).

How Do Fish Have Babies?

To **reproduce,** most female fish lay eggs in the water. Then a male fish of the same **species** swims over the eggs and releases **sperm** over them. When a sperm joins with an egg, the egg is **fertilized** and an **embryo** starts to grow inside it.

Finding a mate

In order to reproduce, fish must find or attract a mate. Some fish use **courtship** displays—colors or movements designed to attract a mate. Male salmon turn from silver to bright colors and develop hook-shaped jaws when it is time to **breed.** Male sticklebacks become more colorful and also do a special dance to encourage a female to lay her eggs.

To attract females, the male three-spined stickleback develops a bright red throat and belly. He builds a nest of weeds and does a zigzag dance to lead females to lay their eggs there.

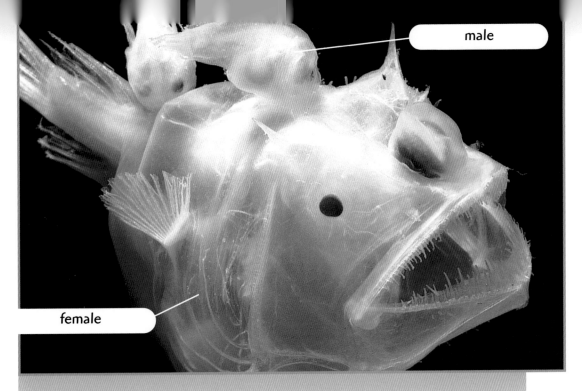

male

female

*In the darkness of the deep sea, the male anglerfish is attracted to a female's lure—the light on her head. He attaches himself to her and lives as a **parasite,** feeding from her **blood supply.** He is always there to breed with her when she is ready.*

Mating territories

Some male fish set up **territories** to mate in. Territories are areas that are good places for laying eggs. Damselfish mostly live around **coral reefs.** A male damselfish makes a territory by clearing seaweed from an area of about 45 to 55 square feet (4 to 5 square meters). He uses courtship displays to attract females ready to mate. He chases away and attacks other males, other types of fish, and sometimes even human divers.

Schools

Fish that live in **schools** do not have to find a mate. The female and male fish simply shed their eggs and sperm at the same time, and fertilization takes place.

Breeding grounds

Male and female fish often meet up to **breed** at the same place year after year. For many species, these places are a shallow part of the pond or river they live in. Others have to make long **migrations.** Adult European eels travel more than 3,100 miles (5,000 kilometers) from rivers, lakes, and ponds where they grew up to certain ocean breeding grounds. Their young return to live in the waters their parents came from.

Breeding seasons

Most fish breed at roughly the same time each year. In cooler parts of the world, most fish **reproduce** in spring or early summer. The water is warmer then so the eggs and young develop more quickly. Also, there is more food around, such as insect **larvae,** for young fish to feed on.

Salmon live in the ocean but return to the rivers they were born in to breed. These salmon are jumping up a waterfall to continue their journey upstream.

Protecting eggs

Many animals like to eat fish eggs, so some fish have ways of hiding their eggs. Some fish lay their eggs in hollows in the sand or gravel at the bottom of a river or pond. They may scoop out the sand with their mouths or flick it away using their tails. Most then cover their eggs with sand to hide them.

Others protect their eggs by staying with them. Seahorses are unusual fish with horse-shaped heads. A female seahorse lays her eggs in a special pouch on the male's front. The eggs remain in the pouch until the young hatch and swim away.

Grunions bury their eggs high up on the beach after the highest tides. The eggs have time to develop and hatch before the next high tide washes them out to sea.

Egg cases

Some fish, such as the dogfish and the bullhead shark, lay just a few eggs. These eggs have a good chance of survival because they are enclosed inside special containers. The cases are tough and protect the embryos inside as they grow. Fish often attach these egg cases to seaweed or rocks to prevent them from being washed away. When the young fish is ready, it breaks out of the case and swims away.

Getting help

Some female fish find others to do the job of protecting their eggs. Bitterlings are river fish. The female has a long egg-laying tube that she uses to lay her eggs inside **shellfish** called mussels. The eggs then develop and hatch safely within the mussel's shell.

Sometimes fish egg cases wash up on the shore after the babies inside have hatched. On the right is a case that contained an egg of the thornback ray.

How Old Do Fish Get?

A living thing's life expectancy is the length of time it is likely to live. Some fish can live for a long time, while others live only a few years. Cod can live for 20 years, and pike can live for up to 50 years. Most fish **species** live for less than 10 years. Sticklebacks live for only 5 years at most.

Most fish never reach their full life expectancy. They, like other animals, can survive only if they find enough food and water and avoid dangers such as fish nets and **predators.** Young and adult fish face many different dangers throughout their lives.

*When adult salmon are about four or five years old, they return to the river where they were born. After mating and laying eggs, they die. They cannot feed in the river and they have no **energy** left for a return trip to the ocean.*

Fish are an important food for millions of people, but careless fishing can endanger many species. Fish nets with small holes catch very young fish. This means there are fewer youngsters to grow up into adults and have young of their own.

Sadly, too many of the colorful fish that live in **habitats** such as this **coral reef** may not make it to adulthood. Pollution, careless use of fish nets, and building on coastlines all threaten the lives of fish in many parts of the world.

The cycle of life

By the time an adult fish dies, it will have left behind many young fish. Some fish lay eggs once or twice each year. So the longer they live, the more likely it is that some of their offspring will survive. A really big mother cod can live for 20 years and lay 10 million eggs every year. This means she could lay hundreds of millions of eggs in a lifetime!

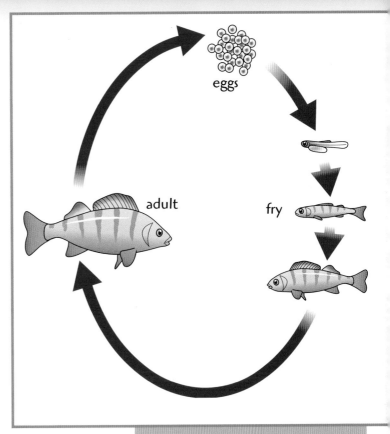

This diagram shows a typical life cycle—a fish fry hatches from an egg, grows into an adult, and has young of its own.

This photo shows a trout laying eggs. Some of the young fish that will hatch from these eggs will eventually become adults, breed, grow old, and die themselves. Their young will continue the cycle.

Fact File

What is . . .

• the largest fish?

The largest fish in the world is the whale shark. It can grow to more than 40 feet (12 meters) long and weigh about 16.5 tons (15 metric tons). That is twice as heavy as an African elephant.

• the smallest fish?

The smallest fish in the world is a goby that lives in the Indian Ocean. It is only $2/5$ inch (1 centimeter) long.

• the oldest fish?

The oldest known fish was a North American lake sturgeon. It was 152 years old when it died.

• the youngest fish?

The shortest-lived fish is the annual fish from South America and Africa. It hatches, grows, **reproduces,** and dies all in less than a year.

A type of goby of the Indian Ocean, shown above, is the smallest fish in the world. This goby is resting on grape coral.

What fish lays the most eggs?

The record for the largest known number of eggs goes to a 5-foot- (1.5-meter-) long cod that laid over 28 million eggs at one time. An average cod lays 7 to 10 million eggs a year.

Fish Classification

Classification is the way scientists group living things together according to features they have in common. Scientists divide all the fish in the world into three main groups.

- Most fish are bony fish. Bony fish have skeletons of bone, flat **scales,** and **gills** protected by gill covers. The biggest group of bony fish is the perchlike fish. There are more than 6,000 different species of perchlike fish, including perch, tuna, mackerel, bass, and gobies.
- The second group is the cartilaginous fish. Cartilaginous fish have a skeleton made of **cartilage,** or gristle. Their scales are pointed, and they have gills slits on either side of the body. Sharks, skates, and rays belong to this group.
- The smallest group is the jawless fish. Jawless fish have no jaws, and their skeletons are soft and made of cartilage. Lampreys and hagfish are jawless fish.

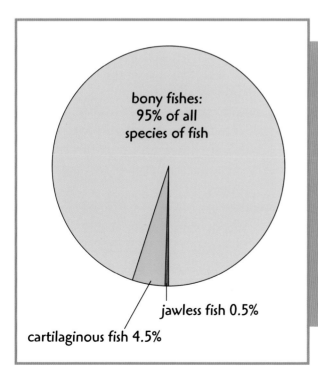

bony fishes:
95% of all
species of fish

jawless fish 0.5%

cartilaginous fish 4.5%

*More than 26,000 **species** of fish are bony fish. Bony fish come in all shapes and sizes—from seahorses to marlin—and live in seas, rivers, and lakes throughout the world. Only one out of every twenty species of fish is cartilaginous or jawless.*

Glossary

barbel soft, thin, whiskerlike feature near the mouth of some kinds of fish

blood supply system of tubes that delivers blood to all parts of the body

breed to have babies

camouflage colors or patterns that help an animal blend in with its background

carnivore meat-eating animal

cartilage support material in animals' bodies that is softer than bone

coral reef giant, rocklike structure made up of the skeletons of millions of tiny reef animals

courtship special behavior that prepares animals for mating

embryo unborn or unhatched young

energy power of living things to do all the activities that they need to do to live and grow

fertilize to cause an egg and sperm to join, which begins the development of an embryo

fin flap or fold of skin that helps fish to swim

fry very young fish

gills body parts used for breathing underwater

habitat place where a plant or animal lives.

larvae young animals that look very different from their parents

migration/migrate seasonal journey of animals to find food or a good place for breeding

muscles parts of the body that help to make the bones and body move

parasite living thing that lives on or inside another living thing, called a host. Parasites get food from the host and may harm it.

plankton tiny animals and plantlike living things that float in water

predator animal that hunts and eats another animal

prey animal that is hunted and eaten by another animal

reproduce when plants and animals make young just like themselves

sac small baglike part on a animal

scale small, flat piece on an animal's skin that is tough like a fingernail

scavenger animal that feeds on dead animals and garbage

school large group of fish of the same kind that live and swim together

shellfish sea animals that live inside shells, such as mussels, oysters, scallops, and crabs

species group of living things that are similar in many ways and can reproduce together to produce healthy babies

sperm small cells produced by male animals that join with eggs to create new young

territory area within a habitat that an animal or group of animals claims as its own. Animals chase uninvited visitors out of their territories.

vertebrates animals with backbones

yolk part of an egg that serves as food for the embryo

More Books to Read

Arnosky, Jim. *All About Sharks.* New York: Scholastic, Inc., 2003.

Jango-Cohen, Judith. *Freshwater Fishes.* Estes Park, Colo.: Benchmark Investigative Group, 2002.

Meish, Goldish. *Salmon and Other Bony Fish.* Chicago, Ill.: World Book, Inc., 2002.

Miller, Sara Swan. *Funny Fishes.* Danbury Conn.: Scholastic Library Publishing, 2001.

Parker, Steve. *Fish.* Bethany, Mo.: Fitzgerald Books, 2001.

Robinson, Fay. *Wacky Fish!* New York: Scholastic, Inc,. 2003.

Scheff, Duncan. *Electric Eels.* Austin, Tex.: Raintree Publishers, 2002.

Slater, Patrick. *Marine Fish.* Broomall, Penn.: Mason Crest Publishers, 2002.

Index